Pebble®
Plus

Cycles of Nature

The Carbon Cycle

A 4D Book

by Catherine Ipcizade

Consultant: Dr. Sandra F. Mather, Professor Emerita
Department of Earth and Space Sciences
West Chester University, West Chester, Pa.

PEBBLE
a capstone imprint

Download the Capstone 4D app!

- Ask an adult to download the Capstone 4D app.

- Scan the cover and stars inside the book for additional content.

When you scan a spread, you'll find fun extra stuff to go with this book! You can also find these things on the web at www.capstone4D.com using the password: carbon.00412

Pebble Plus is published by Pebble
1710 Roe Crest Drive, North Mankato, Minnesota 56003
www.mycapstone.com

Library of Congress Cataloging-in-Publication Data
Names: Ipcizade, Catherine, author.
Title: The carbon cycle : a 4D book / by Catherine Ipcizade.
Description: North Mankato, Minnesota : Pebble, [2019] | Series: Pebble
    plus. cycles of nature | Audience: Ages 4–8.
Identifiers: LCCN 2018002964 (print) | LCCN 2018010032 (ebook) |
    ISBN 9781977100498 (eBook PDF) | ISBN 9781977100412 (hardcover) |
    ISBN 9781977100450 (pbk.)
Subjects: LCSH: Carbon cycle (Biogeochemistry)—Juvenile literature. |
    Carbon—Juvenile literature.
Classification: LCC QH344 (ebook) | LCC QH344 .I74 2018 (print) | DDC
    577/.144—dc23
LC record available at https://lccn.loc.gov/2018002964

Editorial Credits
Emily Raij, editor; Charmaine Whitman, designer;
Eric Gohl, media researcher; Kris Wilfahrt, production specialist

Image Credits
Shutterstock: Daniel Zuppinger, cover (left), 1 (left), Dmytro Zinkevych,
21, John Williams RUS, 5, Oleg Anisimov, 13, Orlando_Stocker, 17, Photo
Design Art, 7, photoiconix, 19, Pinkyone, cover (bottom), 1 (bottom),
RedlineVector, 19 (earth), Sangpeht Surat, 9, Suresh K Srivastava, cover
(right), 1 (right), Tom Wang, 11, Tristan Tan, 15
Design Elements: Shutterstock

Note to Parents and Teachers

The Cycles of Nature set supports the national science standards related to patterns in the natural world. This book describes and illustrates the carbon cycle. The images support early readers in understanding the text. The repetition of words and phrases helps early readers learn new words. This book also introduces early readers to subject-specific vocabulary words, which are defined in the Glossary section. Early readers may need assistance to read some words and to use the Table of Contents, Glossary, Read More, Internet Sites, Critical Thinking Questions, and Index sections of the book.

Printed and bound in China.
309

Table of Contents

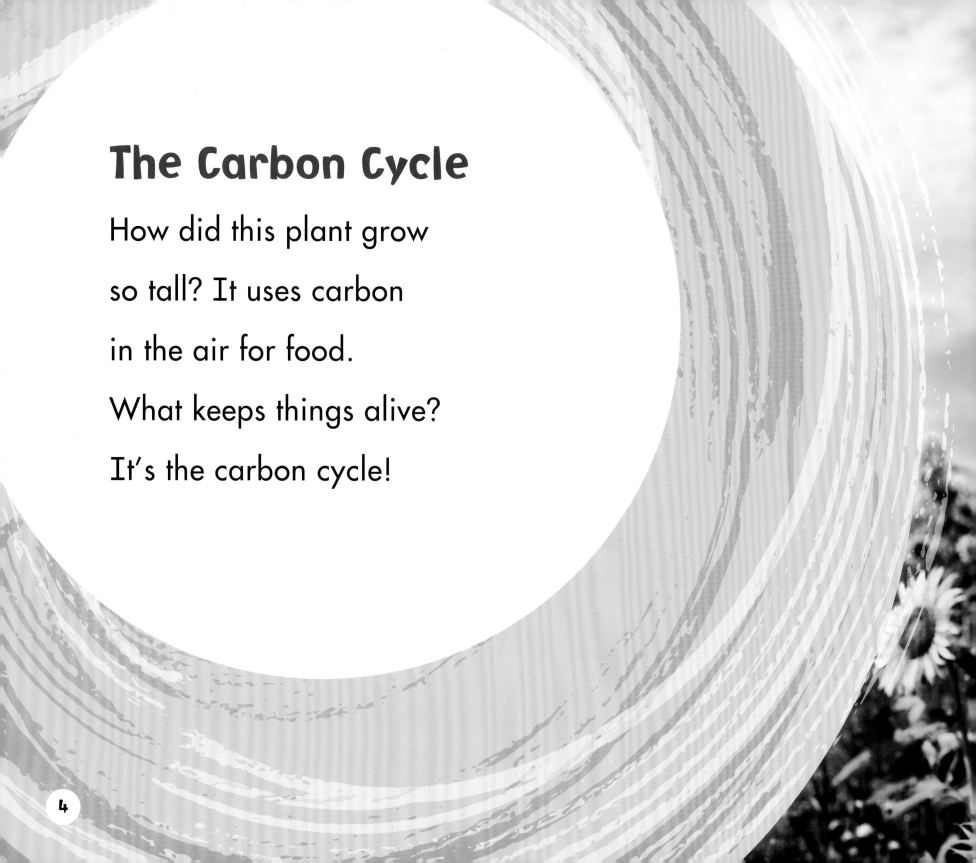

The Carbon Cycle

How did this plant grow
so tall? It uses carbon
in the air for food.
What keeps things alive?
It's the carbon cycle!

4

All living things are made of carbon. People are about 18 percent carbon. Soil, rocks, air, and water have carbon. Carbon is all around us.

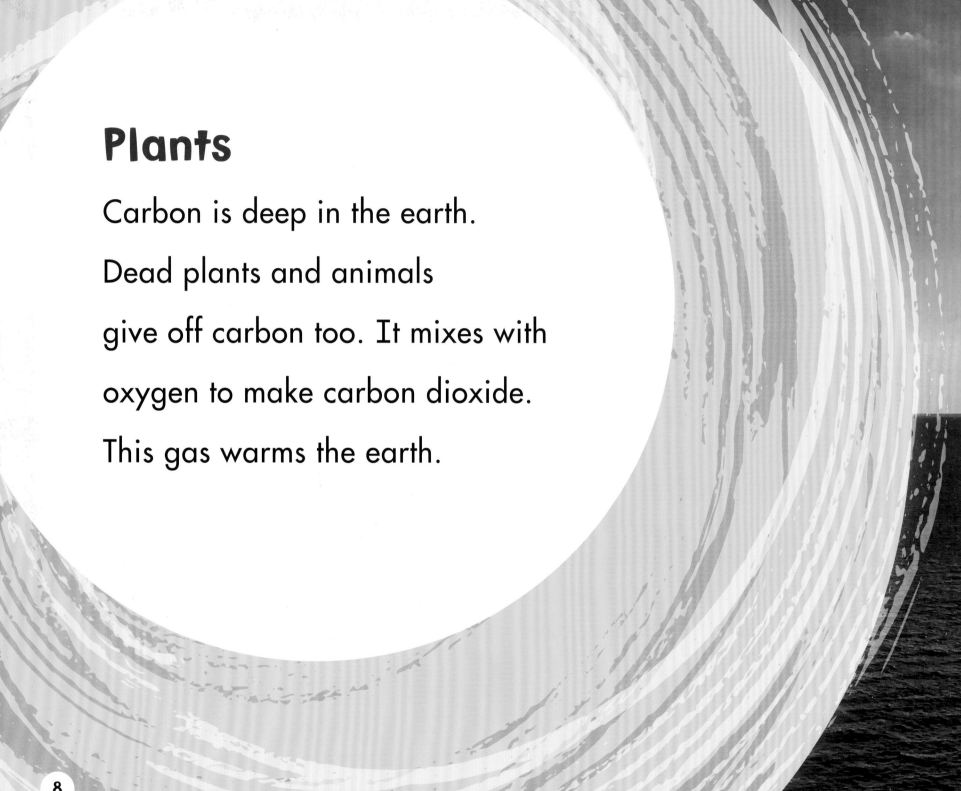

Plants

Carbon is deep in the earth.
Dead plants and animals
give off carbon too. It mixes with
oxygen to make carbon dioxide.
This gas warms the earth.

9

Plants use carbon dioxide
and sunlight to make food.
This process is photosynthesis.
Photosynthesis makes oxygen.

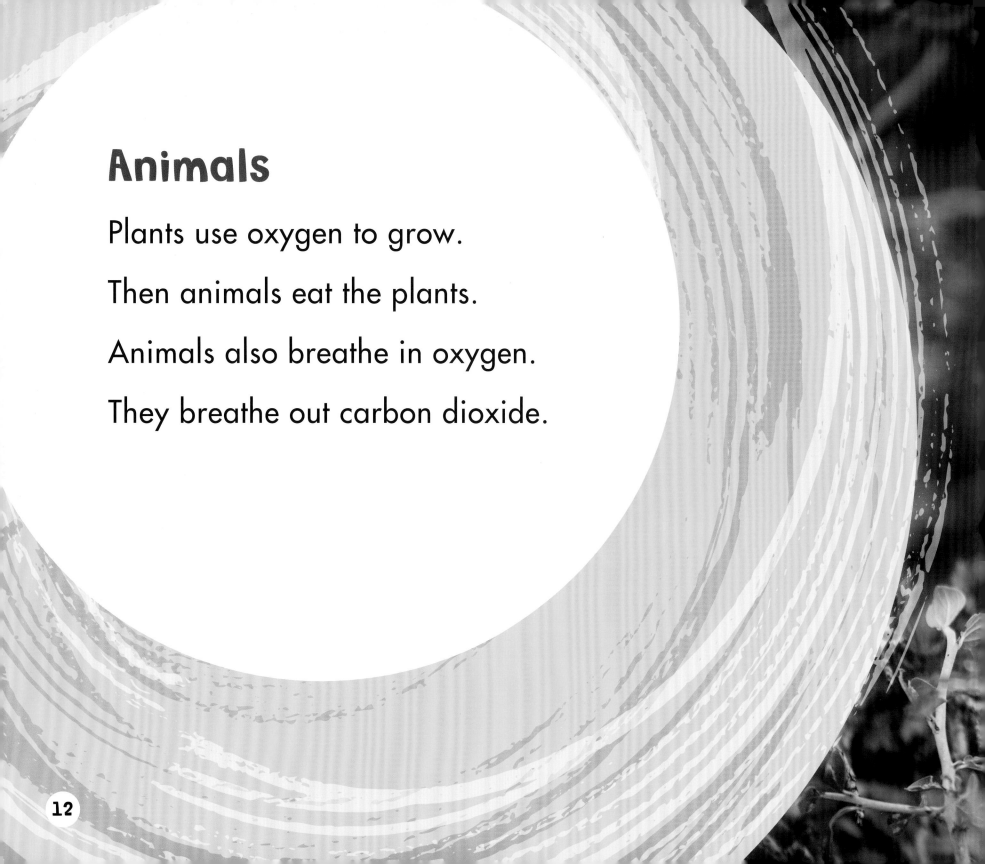

Animals

Plants use oxygen to grow.

Then animals eat the plants.

Animals also breathe in oxygen.

They breathe out carbon dioxide.

13

Fossil Fuels

Dead animals and plants break down into fossil fuels. These fuels are coal, oil, and natural gas. People burn fuel to power cars and make energy.

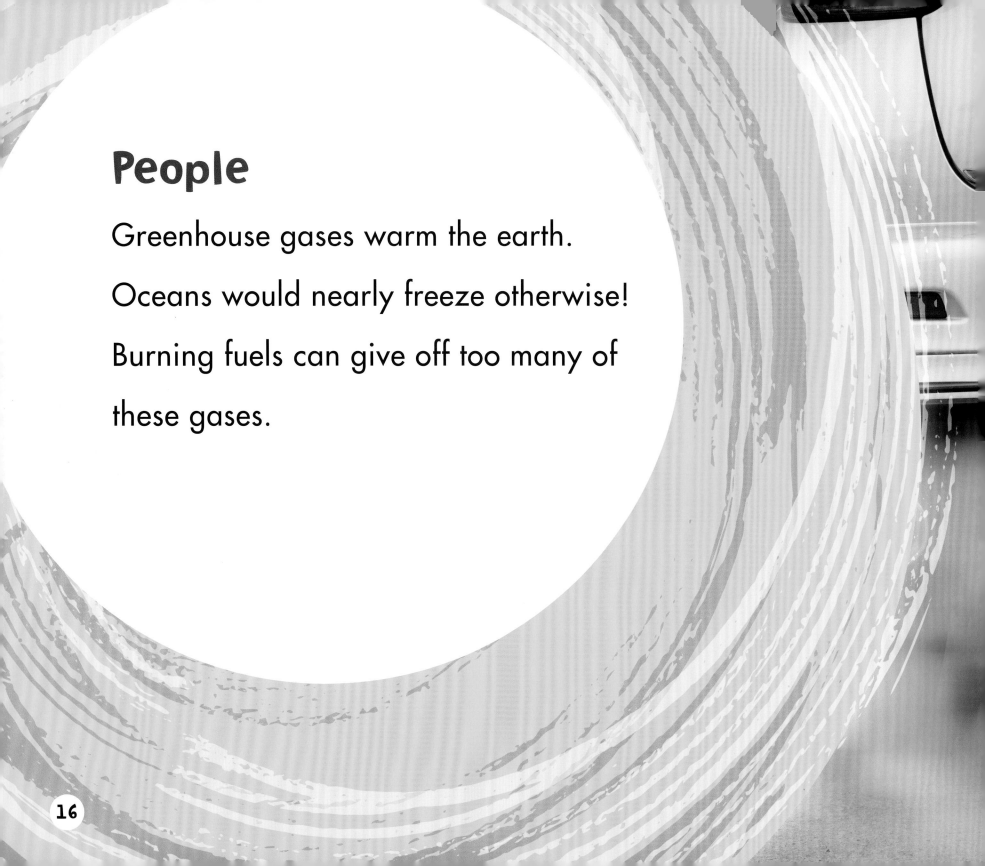

People

Greenhouse gases warm the earth.

Oceans would nearly freeze otherwise!

Burning fuels can give off too many of

these gases.

People burn more fossil fuels than before. This gives off more carbon dioxide than plants and oceans can take out. Temperatures slowly rise. That is global warming.

The Carbon Cycle

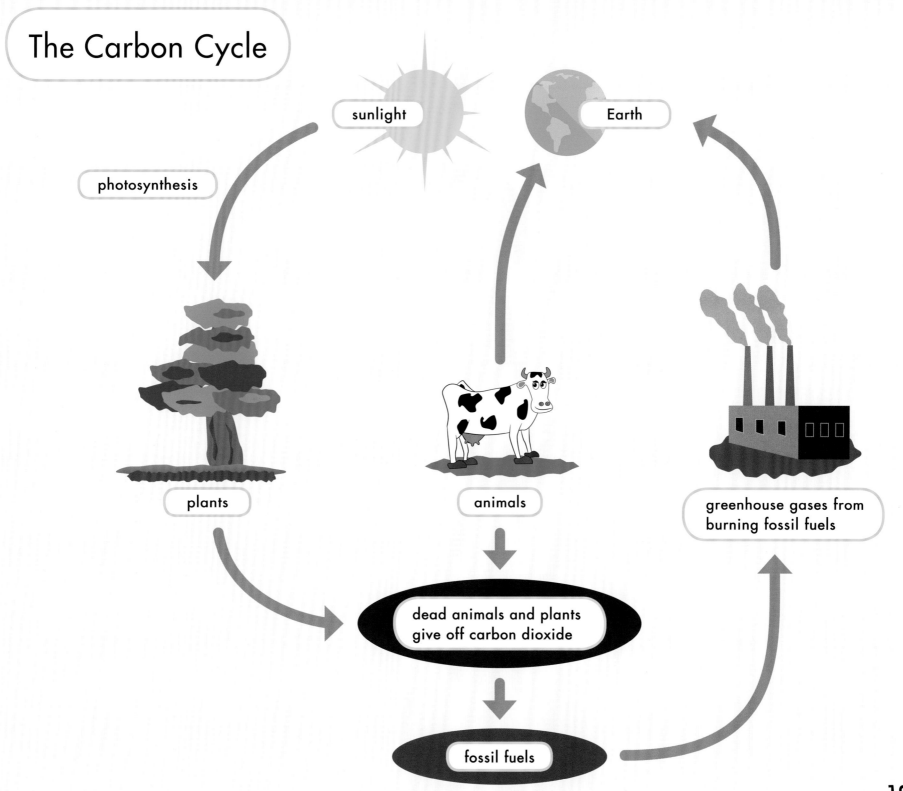

sunlight

Earth

photosynthesis

plants

animals

greenhouse gases from
burning fossil fuels

dead animals and plants
give off carbon dioxide

fossil fuels

19

Too much carbon dioxide
can hurt the earth.
People can use less fuel
and plant more trees.
We can help.

Glossary

carbon dioxide—a gas that has no smell or color; plants take in carbon dioxide because they need it to live.

fossil fuels—natural fuels formed from dead plants and animals; coal, oil, and natural gas are fossil fuels.

global warming—the idea that Earth's temperature is slowly rising

greenhouse gases—gases around the earth that hold in heat

oxygen—a colorless gas that people and animals breathe; people and animals need oxygen to live.

photosynthesis—a process plants use to make food and oxygen

Read More

Dunn, Mary. *A Sunflower's Life Cycle.* Explore Life Cycles. North Mankato, Minn.: Capstone Publishing, 2018.

Loria, Laura. *The Carbon Cycle.* Let's Find Out! New York: Britannica Publishing in Association with Rosen Educational Services, 2018.

Porter, Esther. *Sun Power: A Book about Renewable Energy.* Earth Matters. North Mankato, Minn.: Capstone Publishing, 2013.

Internet Sites

Use FactHound to find Internet sites related to this book.

Visit www.facthound.com

Just type in 9781977100412 and go.

Super-cool stuff! Check out projects, games and lots more at **www.capstonekids.com**

Critical Thinking Questions

1. What kinds of things are made of carbon?

2. How do plants give off oxygen?

3. What can people do to give off less carbon dioxide?

Index